T0171342

The Whole Armor of God
Coat Of Arms

Ephesians 6:10-18

Merry Sonshine

WestBow
PRESS
A DIVISION OF THOMAS NELSON

WestBow Press books may be ordered through booksellers or by contacting:

WestBow Press
A Division of Thomas Nelson
1663 Liberty Drive
Bloomington, IN 47403
www.westbowpress.com
1-(866) 928-1240

Because of the dynamic nature of the Internet, any web addresses or links contained in
this book may have changed since publication and may no longer be valid. The views
expressed in this work are solely those of the author and do not necessarily reflect the
views of the publisher, and the publisher hereby disclaims any responsibility for them.

Any people depicted in stock imagery provided by Thinkstock are models,
and such images are being used for illustrative purposes only.

Certain stock imagery © Thinkstock.

ISBN: 978-1-4497-7989-4 (sc)
ISBN: 978-1-4497-7990-0 (e)

Library of Congress Control Number: 2012923915

Printed in the United States of America

WestBow Press rev. date: 2/27/2013

Table of Content

Table of Contents (continued)

Foreword

By Ronald Ray Fitz-Randolph

Merry and I were married in June of 2004. Merry brought into
My life a greater appreciation for the beauty of nature, and a
Living example of True Faith in God. Merry also brought to our
Marriage a need to complete her book, *The Whole Armor of God.*
She had spent years gathering information about the various
Items of armor, their uses, and developing comparisons with biblical
Equivalents that could be used in the spiritual conflicts we face
In our current daily experiences. She also believes that, as children
Of God, we are Royalty and therefore deserve our own Coat of Arms.
She has devoted much time in developing one.

Merry taught herself how to use Print Shop to prepare the text of
Her book in the style of old time poetry books with borders around
Each page. She also taught herself how to use Adobe Photoshop to
Prepare the Coat of Arms. Merry was diagnosed with Macular
Degeneration in 2001 and in order to create with Adobe Photoshop
She had to use the zoom feature and work with individual pixels. In
July of 2005 fluid behind the retina in her right eye caused it to
Detach and required laser treatment to reattach it. This further
Reduced her vision. In November of the same year she discovered
That she could no longer see yellow. Overcoming the despair this
Caused, she looked into Adobe Photoshop and recorded the numbers
Of each color she used in the Coat Of Arms so she could continue as
She lost more ability to distinguish other colors.

While in Texas in November of 2007, Merry fell and hurt her back.
On the return trip to Wisconsin she passed out several times and
Ended up in the emergency room in Springfield Illinois. It was
Discovered later that she had a torn disk as well as two bulging
Disks. Although she has endured several attempts to relieve the
Pain with injections to the spine, a number of chiropractor visits
And even Some low grade laser treatments, she is still in
Considerable pain and must take morphine for relief. In 2009
Merry was diagnosed as having fibromyalgia which accounted for
Her discomfort throughout her body as well as more than usual.

Pain from a damaged back. Therefore Lyrica was added to her
Medication. In spite of decreasing vision and increasing pain,
Merry was determined that she would complete the book by
Herself. The interruptions, the health issues, all the obstacles
Placed in her way were proof to her that the book was necessary
To help others know about the tools available to fight the constant
Spiritual warfare of today.

With the book cover, the Coat Of Arms, and the text nearly
Complete Merry contacted publishers to determine their
Requirements. She discovered that Print Shop could not be used
To publish her book because of copyright laws, and that she could
Not get a waver. This was spiritual warfare at its worst. The text
Had to be redone in Microsoft Word which required selecting a
New font which changed all the spacing. The border which had
Been selected for its artistic value could not be used. She fought
Off the depression of feeling that the book would never be printed.
She finally decided that it would be better to accept help to
Convert the text and to overcome those things that she was no
Longer able to do. With the publication of this book, my LOVE
Has won her greatest battle.

Ron

Notes from the Author

The intent of this book is to provide the reader with interesting, Secular information about battles fought in ancient times, the Armor that was worn and how this information can be Applied to spiritual battles that Christians face today. (Eph. 6:11)

This comparative study (secular/ Christian) will Use the following format: A "Secular Information" page will be given first, then a "Christian Application" page will follow the Secular Information. This format will continue to the end of Section One.

The historical Coat of Arms was created to identify each family on The battle field. Today, as Christians, we are in the middle of Spiritual Warfare. Our enemy is Satan. Our Christian family Must have identification as well. I have created a Colorful, universal Christian Coat of Arms that will Provide our needed identification. It can be Seen on the back cover of this book.

(If you would like to have a clean color print of this Coat Of Arms to frame and display, identifying Yourself as Christian, the order information Can be found on the last page of this book).

Scripture references are in King James version

Acknowledgements

In 1987, my three teenage sons and their friends were hanging Around my home and one of the girls came inside and wanted to talk. She Said that each morning, she put on the whole armor of God that is listed in Ephesians. I wondered why I shouldn't be doing that too! It became my Daily action and it continues to this day. I want to thank Lori Spitler Oaks For her witness and how it has blessed my life!

Later, I was convicted by the Holy Spirit to put together a book that Would be a comparative study of historical battle information and Spiritual warfare. I studied secular information and God's scriptures and Kept it all in a notebook. I thank the Holy Spirit for the inspiration. I Thank him, also, for all that I have learned, and for the growth that I have Experienced in my faith while I studied for this book.

My husband, Ron (the love of my life) helped me, encouraged me And believed in the book. When I contacted the publisher they told me that I had done the whole book in Print Shop and they wanted it done in Word. Ron chose a plan from the publisher's information and sent the first of Four payments to them. Then he took me for a ride one day and brought Along my book file with my sketches in it. There were two full color Illustrations that I couldn't finish, because I could no longer see colors.

He took me to meet someone very special! (See next paragraph) He Continues to believe in me and the book. I am so blessed to be the recipient Of his love. He, also, demonstrates constant, Christian love when he Relates with me. Thank you, dear one, from the bottom of my heart.

Christy Kopellen (of Printmax Printing, Milton, Wisconsin) used
My sketches and color choices to create a new level of quality for the book.
(She made the front and back covers come to life!)
Thanks so much Christy!
Then Paul and Christine Snyder came to visit and told me that
They would move the text from Print Shop to Word. They worked long
Hours until it was done. Because my vision ability had diminished
Considerably, they helped me when I could not finish the book.
Thank you both so much!
One real joy for me was meeting Rabbi Andrea Steinberger of the
Hills Foundation at the University of Madison Wisconsin. She gave me the
Exact hebrew marks for the bottom right-hand quarter of the shield in the
Newly created Christian Coat of Arms. Thank you Rabbi Steinberger.
It was indeed a pleasure to meet you!

Thanks also to those who looked for Spelling
And punctuation errors: Sandy Kutz, Joshua, Sarah,
Anni, Becky, Shanny and Lydiah Snyder, NolaMae Gray,
Sherry Derr and my son, Dr. Michael J. Fansler.

Romans 1:8

"First, I thank my God through

Jesus Christ for you all."

Section One

The Armor

(Secular Information and Christian Application)

<u>Introduction</u> -Secular Information

$\mathscr{I}$n the very early years, war was a daily

Fact of life. Although great armies engaged

In battle against each other, in truth the

Fight was really won or lost between two

Individuals who fought in the armies, one trying to

Defeat the other. In order to protect oneself while

In battle, elaborate clothing and armor was

Created to protect the fighter's body. So much

Protection was needed that a person became

Encased in a heavy suit of armor.

<u>Introduction</u> - Christian Application

"Put on the whole armor of God."
Ephesians 6:11

Spiritual warfare is a daily fact of life.

Although the warfare is between God and Satan and

Their armies, the battle - so often - comes down to a

Contest between two individuals: the child of God

(Christian) and Satan (God's enemy).

How does one protect

Oneself while engaged in spiritual battle?

What armor would provide protection for the spirit?

We will find the answers in the

Word of God.

Identification – Secular Information

A full suit of armor, though it did protect the warrior,
Made it impossible for the warrior to be recognized. To keep friend
From wounding friend, it became necessary for each person to be
Identifiable while wearing the armor. The first identifier was the
Surname (The father's family name), which was indicated on the
Shield. Surnames evolved from several general sources.
Examples:

Father's name:

(If Peter's son was James, he was "James Peterson")

Occupation:

(If Robert baked bread, he was "Robert Baker")

Where he lived:

(If George lived on a hill, he was "George Hill")

Physical Features:

(If John had black hair, his name was "John Black")

Symbols (Objects that represent something) were used as artistic
Renderings of someone's name. For example, many of the
Fisher's arms used the symbol of a fish to represent their name.
Symbols might also represent ideals such as hope and
Joy. A religious symbol represented Faith.

Identification - Christian Application

"One God and Father of all."

Ephesians 4:6

When we move through our lives today, things can be
Confusing. How do we know who is of God and who is enemy?
We need to create some way of identifying ourselves as children of God.
Using history as our model, our first and most important
Identifier should come from our Father's name.
We call ourselves "Christians."
This name was developed in a very specific way:

God: Our Spiritual Father (Matthew 23:9)
"For one is your Father, which is in heaven"

Jesus Christ: God in the flesh (John 10:30)
"I and my Father are one."

Man: We are created by Him (Genesis 1:27)
"Male and female created he them."

Christians: Children of God, through Christ (John 1:12)
*"But as many as received him, to them gave he power to
Become the sons of God."*

There was a symbol that was used by the early Christians as a means to
Identify themselves as followers of Jesus: it was the fish.   The symbol
Was drawn in the sand pointing to where the other Christians
Could be found. Later, Greek letters were placed inside
The fish. They said: "Jesus Christ,
Son of God, Savior."

Crest – Secular Information

*T*he Crest was an ornament that was attached to the top of the helmet
At the very highest point. It was usually made of feathers or thin
Metal and was attached to the helmet with studs.

Having a Crest on the helmet demonstrated the following:

It showed hereditary distinction
(It was his father's crest)

It identified superior standing
(It served as a mark of rank)

It was a symbol of courage
(The warrior was willing to go into battle)

It deflected the blows of the enemy.
(The blow meant for the head was intercepted)

The Crest usually survived the battle when the helmet
And shield were destroyed. The remaining
Crest then became a rallying point
Around which the followers gathered.

Crest - Christian Application

"He that cometh from above is above all."
John 3:31

*W*ebster defines Crest as *"The highest level."* In the spiritual Battle, the one who is at the highest level is Jesus Christ (King of Kings). He was exalted and given *"A Name Which is above every name."* (Philippians 2:9)

Having Christ as one's Savior provides the following:

<u>Hereditary distinction</u> (Galatians 4:7)
"Wherefore thou art no more a servant, but a son."

<u>Superior standing</u> (Ephesians 2:6)
"And hath raised us up together, and made us sit Together in heavenly places in Christ Jesus."

<u>A symbol of courage - The Cross</u> (John 19:17)
"And he bearing his cross went forth into...Golgotha."

<u>Deflected blows of the enemy</u> (1 Peter 2:24)
"By whose stripes ye were healed."

They tried to destroy the Gospel on the cross.
However, Christ rose from the grave and
He, *"our highest level"*, remains the
Rallying point around which
His followers gather.

Helmet - Secular Information

The Helmet was a protective covering for the head and was
Placed directly below the Crest. The rank of the one
Wearing the helmet corresponded with the
Type of helmet that was worn. Royalty,
For example, wore brass helmets
With brass bars on the visor.

The head (mind) of a warrior was used to do the following:

Understand the enemy.
(Learn how he thinks)

Acquire knowledge.
(Learn the truth about him)

Plan a strategy.
(To take him captive)

Helmet - Christian Application

"Take the helmet of salvation."
Ephesians 6:17

Our helmet is below the Crest; Jesus Christ - God in the flesh.
The helmet of salvation reflects our standing with our heavenly
Father: "I will receive you, and will be a Father unto you and ye shall be
My sons and daughters saith the Lord Almighty" (II Corinthians 6:17b -18).
Our salvation through Christ's sacrifice places us in the position of being
Members of a royal family. The most effective weapon that
Satan can use against us in spiritual warfare is
To attack our inner thoughts.

Our helmet of salvation protects our minds, enabling
Us to do the following:
Understand the enemy (John 8:44b)
"For he is a liar, and the father of it."

Acquire knowledge (John 18:37)
"For this cause came I into the world, that I should bear
Witness unto the truth. Every one that is of the truth
Heareth my voice."

Plan a strategy (II Corinthians 10:5b)
"Bringing into captivity every thought"

Mantling - Secular Information

Webster defines a mantle as a loose outer garment. It was
Usually made of velvet and was attached to the
Top of the helmet. It then draped down the
Back and sides to frame the helmet,
The warrior and his shoulders.

Wearing a mantle provided the following:

A covering during storms.
(Keeping the warrior dry)

Protection from the hot sun.
(Metal armor can get very hot)

It entangled the enemy's sword.
(Rendering it useless)

Mantling - Christian Application

"He hath covered me with the robe of righteousness."
Isaiah 61:10

The Bible has many verses about long, loose garments.
Some are called robes, others are raiment or cloaks.
Matthew 9:20-21 illustrates Christ wearing such a robe:
"And, behold, a woman, which was diseased with
An issue of blood twelve years, came behind him, and
Touched the hem of his garment: For she said within herself,
If I may but touch his garment, I shall be whole."

Christ's Mantle of Righteousness provides us with the following:

A covering during storms: (Isaiah 4:6b)
"And for a place of refuge, and for a covert
From storm and from rain."

Protection from the fire: (Isaiah 43:2b)
"When thou walkest through the fire,
Thou shalt not be burned."

It entangles the enemy's weapons: (Ephesians 6:16b).
Ye shall be able to quench all the fiery darts of the wicked."

Breastplate - Secular Information

The breastplate was the earliest piece of body armor worn in battle.
At the beginning, it was crafted into a basic metal piece. It
Evolved into an elaborate and decorative creation as time passed.
It was worn on the front of the body as a protective covering for the
Heart. It was attached to another plate that covered the warrior's back.
"Stop ribs" were placed at the edges of the breastplate nearest to
The neck and arm areas to prevent the sword blade from
Skipping off and wounding the warrior.
The breastplate was an effective protective covering.

When it was worn:
The warrior was safe
(It stopped the sword)

The warrior's heart was protected
(From the enemy's blows)

The warrior was not vulnerable
(Enabling him to stand firm)

The one who used the breastplate had the responsibility of inspecting it,
Maintaining it, keeping it in good repair and ready for battle.

Breastplate - Christian Application

"Having on the breastplate of righteousness."

Ephesians 6:14

The translation for righteousness is *"A condition acceptable to God"*
(For Christians - it is through Christ). Ephesians chapter 6 lists the
Breastplate of righteousness as the second piece of armor to put on,
Establishing its importance in spiritual warfare.
When it is worn on the front of the body, its purpose is to guard the
Heart which is the seat of a persons' emotions, self-worth and trust. As
In secular battle, the breastplate is needed when facing the enemy.
It is also an effective protective covering!

When worn, the following is true:

The Christian is safe (Psalms 91:5)
"Thou shalt not be afraid for the...arrow that flieth by day."

The Christian is protected (II Chronicles 16:9)
*"For the eyes of the Lord run to and fro throughout the
Whole earth, to shew himself strong in the behalf of
Them whose heart is perfect toward him."*

The Christian is not vulnerable (Isaiah 41:10)
*"Fear thou not...I will uphold thee with the
Right hand of my righteousness."*

We must take good care of our breastplate of righteousness,
Wearing it daily, inspecting and maintaining it. It must
Reflect the glory of God and be ready for battle.

<u>Belt</u> - Secular Information

The belt (sometimes called a girdle) was made more like an apron. It was
The belt that kept the loins girded (encircled) around the waist
(Between the bottom of the ribs and the top of the hips).

It was important for the following reasons:

<u>It held the person's tunic in place</u>
(Making it easier to freely move around)

<u>It served as a strap for the breastplate</u>
(Holding it in place against the warrior's body)

<u>It was used to hold the sword</u>
(Keeping it available and ready for use)

Without the belt to hold them in place, all other components
Would come apart. Loose armor could cause problems in
Battle, so it was important that the warrior
Properly placed and secured the belt.

<u>Belt</u> - Christian Application

"Stand therefore, having your loins girt about with truth."
Ephesians 6:14

*I*n this scripture, the belt of truth is listed first,
Suggesting its importance.

We must put on our belt for the following reasons:

<u>It surrounds the Christian with truth</u>
(John 14:6) *"I (Jesus) am the way, the truth and the life."*

<u>It holds righteousness securely in place</u> (II Corinthians 6:7)
*"By the word of truth, by the power of God, by the
Armour of righteousness."*

<u>It keeps the sword of the Spirit ready for use</u> (II John 1:2)
*"For the truth's sake, which dwelleth in us, and shall
Be with us for ever."*

If we are not encompassed by truth (Jesus) at all
Times, our lives will most surely fall apart.
This belt is not put on for us.
We must put it on ourselves.

<u>Shield</u> - Secular Information

It could not be assumed that a person might have the
Privilege of carrying a shield. It was an honor that was
Granted to worthy people in good standing by the King of
Armor - the Senior Herald – who acted with royal
Authority. Royalty used shields that were
Made of pounded brass.

The following was true about a shield:

<u>It was a solid, flat piece of metal or wood</u>
(It could be trusted in battle)

<u>It protected the warrior</u>
(It was relied on to ward off blows)

<u>It was the most important piece of armor</u>
(Enabling the fighter to overcome the enemy)

<u>It was durable</u>
(The fighter endured many difficult battles)

Since the shield was the central element of all armor, it was
Important that it had a good balance between
Ease of use and reliability.

<u>Shield</u> - Christian Application

"Above all, taking the shield of faith."

Ephesians 6:16

*I*t is an honor for us to carry our shield of faith. It cannot be assumed. The privilege is granted because Jesus Christ (Our Herald) proclaims that His sacrifice put us in good standing with the highest authority (God).

The following is true about our shield of faith:

<u>It is solid through trust in the Lord</u> (Psalms 144:2)
"My goodness, and my fortress; my high tower, and my Deliverer; my shield, and he in whom I trust."

<u>It protects the Christian</u> (Psalms 28:7)
"The Lord is my strength and my shield; my heart trusted in Him, and I am helped."

<u>It is the most important piece of armor</u> (Proverbs 30:5)
"He is a shield unto them that put their trust in him."

<u>It is durable</u> (Isaiah 9:6b)
We are all children of God by faith in Jesus Christ-"And his name Shall be called...The everlasting Father." (Everlasting, translated From the Greek word, means "duration/constancy").

Faith is the central element of all our spiritual armor. It must
Be balanced between our faithful and
Steadfast reliance on
Our trustable God.

<u>Supporters</u> - Secular Information

A brief explanation of history and supporters would tell us that a Knight was one who was chosen and formally trained for high military Rank. The required qualities for a knight were bravery, honorable Behavior, a display of respectful attitude, honesty and courtesy. (A knight went into battle mounted on a horse).

Before they became knights, two stages of training were required:

Ages 8 - 14 (Their title was "Page"). Training included:

<u>Education</u>

<u>Religion</u>

<u>Military</u>

<u>Cultural</u>

Ages 15 - 20 (Their title was "Squire"). Training included:

<u>Methods of Serving</u>

<u>Armor/weapon maintenance</u>

<u>Preparing the knight for battle</u>

<u>Learning the use of armor/weapons</u>

<u>How to be a supporter during battle</u>

(The squire went into battle on foot staying beside the Knight, addressing his needs as they arose).

High Rank position (Their title was "Knight"). The process:

<u>The squire knelt down</u>

<u>A lord or king touched each shoulder with a sword</u>

<u>The squire was then dubbed to be a knight</u>

<u>The knight was given supporters (squires)</u>

(Who would be of service on and

Off the battlefield)

<u>Supporters</u> - *Christian Application*

"Are they (angels) not all ministering spirits, sent forth to minister?"
Hebrews 1:14

A brief history on how we became Christians would show that we
Were chosen (2 Timothy 2:4), then formally trained for high rank
(2 Timothy 2:15). Some of the qualities that a Christian develops are:
Honorable behavior, respectful attitude, courage, obedience and
Kindness. Before we become mature Christians, ready for battle,
We are required to go through periods of training:

As Young children, our training includes:
<u>Education</u> (Proverbs 22:6)
    "Train up a child in the way he should go...he will not
    Depart from it."
<u>Christian behavior</u> (Galatians 5: 22 - 23)
    The fruits of the spirit are listed therein
<u>Knowledge</u> (2 Peter 1:5)
    "And besides this, giving all diligence, add to your faith
    Virtue; and to virtue knowledge."
<u>God's instruction</u> (Exodus 20:3 -17/Mark 12:30-31)
    "Thou shalt have no other gods before me," etc. / "Love the Lord
    Thy God with all thy heart, and with all thy soul, and
    With all thy mind, and with all thy strength...
    Love thy neighbor as thyself."
As young adults, our training includes:
<u>Servanthood</u> (Proverbs 14:35)
    "The king's favor is toward a wise servant."
<u>Use/maintenance of armor</u> (Jeremiah 46:4b)
    "Stand forth with *your* helmets; furbish the spears."
<u>Helping others to prepare for battle</u> (1 Thessalonians 5:17)
    "Pray without ceasing."
<u>Supporting others during spiritual battles</u> (James 5:16)
    "The effectual fervent prayer of a righteous man
    Availeth much."
High Rank Position: Our new title, is "Warrior." We then:
<u>Kneel before our Lord and King</u>. (Psalms 95:6)
    "Let us kneel before the Lord our maker."
<u>Are touched with His sword of truth</u> (John 17:17)
    "Sanctify them through thy truth: thy Word is truth."
<u>Have a new name: Christian Warrior</u> (Revelation 2:17b).
    "To him that overcometh will I give...a new name."
        <u>Are given powerful supporters</u>
    (Luke 4:10) "He shall give his angels
    Charge over thee, to keep thee."

Foot Coverings - Secular Information

The warriors wore sandals that had spikes or hobnails on the soles

Which provided good balance even on rough terrain. The uppers

Of the sandals were made with open weaving of lightweight

Leather, enabling the warrior to march or stand for

Long periods of time. The leather straps were

Placed so they wouldn't cause blisters.

These sandals were called "Caliagae"

(Cal'-i-guy), translated

As "little boots."

Caliagae were designed for the following purposes:

To wear while in battle

(Waging war)

Standing firm during combat

(A difficult task, when in battle)

Comfort while on foot

(Welcome during combat)

<u>Foot Coverings</u> - Christian Application

"And your feet shod with the preparation of the gospel of peace."
Ephesians 6:15

" Your feet shod with the preparation of the gospel of peace."
Ephesians 6 tells us to stand. The example of the Caliagae sandals
Shows that our hobnails (memorized scriptures) will enable us to
Stand immovable - even in rough places. Caliagae were also
Comfortable and lightweight for long marches. Our
Spiritual shoes make it easier for us to stand
Firm in the face of the enemy.

Wearing spiritual Caliagae enables us to do the following:

<u>*Engage in warfare with confidence*</u> *(II Corinthians 10:4)*
"For the weapons of our warfare are not carnal, but
Mighty, through God."

<u>*Stand firmly while in battle*</u> *(1 Peter 5:12)*
"The true grace of God wherein ye stand."

<u>*Be comfortable while we stand*</u> *(Ephesians 2:14)*
"For he is our peace." (Calm)

Sword - Secular Information

Swords were probably the first tools designed just for
War. They began as broadswords that were six to eight feet long.
Two hands were required to swing it in wide
Sweeps in an attempt to slash an attacker. This action left the
Fighter wide open for the enemy to move in and strike.
Later, a more efficient sword was developed.
It was called a Thrusting sword.

Facts about the thrusting sword are listed below:

It was sharp.
(On two edges)

It was used to thrust.
(Straight into the attacker)

Practice was required.
(To perfect ability to use it)

It was always available.
(Within the warrior's reach)

<u>Sword</u> - Christian Application

"Take...the sword of the Spirit, which is the word of God."

Ephesians 6:17

The sword of the spirit is an offensive tool, designed to be Effective in spiritual warfare. <u>It is the word of God</u>. There are two different Greek words used in the Bible to translate "Word": One is "logos", which means the written word of God. The other is "Rhema", and it refers to repeating the sayings of God and Applying them to certain - applicable situations as they arise in Our lives. In Ephesians 6:17, The Greek word "rhema" is used.

Facts about the word of God are listed below:

<u>It is sharp</u> *(Hebrews 4:12)*
"For the word of God is quick, and powerful, And sharper than any two-edged sword."

<u>It cuts to the heart</u> *(Hebrews 4:12)*
"Piercing even to the dividing asunder Of soul and spirit."

<u>Practice is required</u> *(I Peter 2:2)*
"As newborn babes, desire the sincere Milk of the word, that ye may grow thereby."

<u>It is always available</u> *(Psalms 119:11)*
"Thy word have I hid in mine heart."

Rights To An Identification Design – Secular Information

Once the surname was verified, rights to a personal, artistic
Identification design was granted. The design was then
Created and recorded in the Book of Records, which was held
By the King of Arms. In order for someone to be granted a
Right to an artistic identification
Design and have it recorded, that person was required
To have the following qualifications:

He must be a DIRECT descendant
(Webster) To be derived from birth.

He must be a LEGITIMATE descendant
(Webster) To maintain as truth.

He must be a PROVEN descendant
(Webster) To ascertain as fact by evidence.

These qualifications must come from the male line of someone
To whom the right of identification was previously
Granted and was written in the
Book of Records.

Rights To An Identification Design – Christian Application

"And there shall in no wise enter in…but they which are written
In the Lamb's book of life."
Revelation 21:27

"Christian" is our spiritual surname if we are followers of Christ.
We look to the scriptures to find our qualifying rights to use that name.
Our new name will be listed in the Lamb's book of life that is held by
Jesus Christ, The King of Kings. In order for someone
To be granted a right to an identification design
And have it recorded in the Lamb's book of life, that person must
Have the following qualifications:

He must be a direct descendant (1 John 5:1)
"Whosoever believeth that Jesus is the Christ is
Born of God."

He must be a legitimate descendant (Romans 8:14)
"For as many as are led by the Spirit of God, they
Are the sons of God."

He must be a proven descendant - (Romans 8:16)
"The Spirit itself beareth witness with our spirit, that
We are the children of God."

Our qualifications come from the spiritual line of Jesus Christ, whose
Rights to His own identification design are
Written in God's book of records.

Knowledge - Secular Information

Wearing even the finest armor that was available did
Not guarantee a victory in battle. One also needed to have
A solid knowledge in regard to the enemy. Webster's dictionary
Gives the following definitions for the word "Knowledge":

Direct perception
"To obtain straightforward
Information through the senses"
(See, hear and feel).

Information
Who is he?
What is his goal?
What strategies does he use?
What is his weakness?

Understanding
Grasping the significance
Of the enemy.

Knowledge - Christian Application

"The heart of him that hath understanding seeketh knowledge."
Proverbs 15:14

Ephesians 6: 11 - 17 tells us about some of God's spiritual Armor we should wear. However, we must do more! We must Acquire knowledge about our enemy. Knowledge, described below, Will prepare us for effective spiritual battle.

Direct perceptions (Matthew 7:20)
"Wherefore by their fruits ye shall know them."
 (See, hear and feel the results of Satan's actions)

Accumulated facts (Information about Satan)
Who is he? (Ephesians 6:12) The ruler of darkness.
What is his goal? (John 10:10) To kill, steal and destroy us.

What are his strategies? (John 8:44) He is a liar.
What is his weakness? (James 4:7) *"Submit yourselves Therefore to God. Resist the devil, and he will flee from you."*
He flees from God's presence.

Understanding the enemy's significance - (I Peter 5:8).
"Be sober, be vigilant; because your adversary the Devil, as a roaring lion, walketh about, seeking Whom he may devour."

Practice - Secular Information

Jousting (engaging in practice combat) was developed to provide The warrior with the opportunity to retain and refine accurate fighting Skills. It was a practice of defending oneself and developing Offensive skills in order to defeat the opponent.

Here are a few ways that Webster defines "Practice":

Habit - Repetitive actions.
(Doing it over and over)

Training - Learning self-control.
(Exercising influence on self)

Exercise - To put in motion.
(A state of active functioning)

Action - To exert energy
(Power displayed)

... And so they often entered the field for practice.

<u>Practice</u> – Christian Application

"Be ye doers of the word, and not hearers only."

James 1:22

To retain our ability to resist the devil, we must exercise our Techniques of defense. Our offensive tool is the sword - the word Of God. If we study and memorize it, we will be Prepared for the enemy's attacks.

Here are a few ways we can practice for spiritual warfare:

<u>Habit</u> - (Isaiah 34:16)

"Seek ye out of the book of the Lord and read."

<u>Training</u> - (Titus 2:7)

"In all things shewing thyself a pattern of good works."

<u>Exercise</u> - (I Timothy 4:7)

"Exercise thyself rather unto godliness."

<u>Action</u> - (Jeremiah 23:29)

"Is not my word...like a hammer that breaketh the Rock into pieces?"

... And so, Christian, we must often enter
The field for practice

Announcement! - Secular Information

The trumpet sounded as two individuals entered the field for practice.
At that time, the herald announced the following information:

The person's surname
(His significant achievements and his
Position in the family)

His father's name
(His significant achievements and his
Position in the family)

The name of his father's father
(His significant achievements and his
Position in the family)

Once the announcements were made, the two individuals entered
The field and began perfecting their battle skills. This
Process was needed so they could be prepared
For the moment when they were
Called to real battle.

<u>Announcement!</u> - *Christian Application*

"He that overcomes...I will confess his name before

My Father, and before his angels."

Revelation 3:5

The trumpet sounds as we enter the field for practice, and our

Herald announces the following information:

<u>Christian</u>

A Soldier of Christ ("As a good soldier of Jesus Christ" -II Timothy 2:3).

An adopted child of God ("The adoption of children by

Jesus Christ." - Ephesians 1:5).

<u>*Redeemed by -*</u>

<u>Jesus Christ</u>

Who died on the cross ("He humbled himself, and became obedient unto

Death, even the death of the cross." (Philippians 2:8) He rose from the dead

("...He rose again the third day" - I Corinthians 15:4).

<u>*The only begotten son of -*</u>

<u>God Almighty</u>

Creator of: ("The heavens, the earth and the seas" - Nehemiah 9:6).

Our Heavenly Father ("Our Father which art in heaven' - Matthew 6:9").

The Alpha and the Omega ("I am...the beginning and the ending." (Rev1: 8).

Entering the practice field provides the child of God with the opportunity

To perfect needed battle skills. This practice is important because

It prepares the warrior for the moment

When the enemy launches a

Real attack.

The Call To Battle – Secular Information

The person in charge of the warriors called them together so he could
Give them orders and lay out his plan. He began by explaining why it
Was necessary for them to go into battle. Then he named the enemy and
Told them about the damage that the enemy was causing. After
That, he put a challenge to all those who followed him: "Make sure that
Your armor is in place and secure, be ready for difficult times, be
Aware and watch at all times for the presence of the enemy." He
Explained they would be going into the midst of the enemy's camp,
And said that every person they protected would be saved from death.
He was emphatic that he didn't want to lose even one person!.
Each soldier was instructed to put away all thoughts pertaining to
Anything but the battle while in combat. They needed to be completely
Committed to the cause for which they fought. He reassured his soldiers
That he would go into battle before them and would not forsake them.
Finally, he promised that they would be
Rewarded upon their victory.

The Call To Battle - Christian Application
"Fight the good fight of faith"

I Timothy 6:12

God calls us together so he can give us orders and lay out His plan:
"Come you who has ears and hear me (Matthew 11:15). Difficult and fierce
Times have come in these days and people are being pulled away
From the knowledge of God's truth (II Timothy 3:1 - 7)
Because Satan is transformed into an angel of light
(II Corinthians 11:14) as he walks about seeking whom
He may destroy (I Peter 5:8). He is the ruler of the darkness of this
World (Ephesians 6:12). Put on the whole armor of God that you
May be able to stand against the wiles of the devil (Ephesians 6:11)
And endure hardness as a good soldier (II Timothy 2:3). Be sober. Be
Vigilant (1 Peter 5:8). Behold, I send you forth as lambs among the
Wolves (Luke 10:3). Go ye into all the world (Mark 16:15) and proclaim
As heralds the good news. He who converts the sinner from the
Error of his way shall save a soul from death (James 5:20).
I am not willing that any should Perish (II Peter 3:9).
Do not tangle yourself with the affairs of this life. Warfare requires
Entire concentration (II Timothy 2:4). I will never leave nor
Forsake you (Hebrews 13:5). I will be your shield (Proverbs 30:5).
To him who overcometh, I will grant to
Sit with me in my throne".

(Revelation 3:21)

Romans 8:37 – 39

"Nay, in all these things we are more

Than conquerors through him that loved us.

For I am persuaded, that neither death, nor

Life, nor angels, nor principalities, nor

Powers, nor things present, nor things to

Come, nor height, nor depth, nor any other

Creature, shall be able to separate

Us from the love of God, which

Is in Christ Jesus our Lord."

Philippians 4:13

"*I* can do all things

Through Christ

Which strengtheneth me."

The Moment- Physical Battle

Now, the moment has come! The warrior must face the Enemy. What thoughts are racing through his mind?

<u>I'm so afraid!</u>
I've got to overcome this fear!
I need to remember to be brave!
I must think good thoughts!

<u>Will I die?</u>
I must fight the enemy!
I don't want to die!
I <u>MUST</u> be brave!

<u>Will I be victorious?</u>
How do I gain victory?
Who is able to help me get victory?
I need to find someone to help me!

When "the moment" comes,
When a deep breath has been drawn,
The warrior finds courage when surrounded
By other soldiers as they follow
Their leader's commands

The Moment- Spiritual Battle

When does "the moment" come for a Christian?
Does it stand boldly before a person or does it sneak
Into one's mind and life in a subtle manner?

What thoughts run through ones mind when "the moment"
Suddenly becomes recognized?
<u>I am so afraid!</u>
(Romans 8:31) "What shall we then say to these
Things? If God be for us, who can be against us?"

<u>Will I die?</u>
(Matthew 10:28) "And fear not them which kill
The body, but are not able to kill the soul; but
Rather fear him which is able to destroy both
Soul and body in hell."

<u>Will I be victorious?</u>
(I Corinthians 15:57) "But thanks be to God,
Which giveth us the victory through our
Lord Jesus Christ."

When "the moment" is clearly apparent, a deep breath is taken,
And the motto is shouted! The Christian warrior then falls
Into formation behind his trustable leader (The Lord)
And marches toward the enemy.
He whispers a heartfelt prayer

Motto – Secular Information

Webster defines "Motto" as a principle of behavior. Along with the
Artistic identification design (Coat of Arms), a motto was
Used. Some family mottos were war cries that expressed
Pious, loyal, or moral sentiment. Others stood
For hope or determination. There were also
Those that reflected fierceness.

The Following is an example of a motto:

"MY BLOOD FOR MY COUNTRY!"

Once the warrior was prepared, he shouted
Out his motto and marched into battle.

Motto - Christian Application

"We are more than conquerors through him that loved us"
Romans 8:37

Principle, defined by Webster, is a fundamental truth guided by
Certain rules of conduct. A motto that is placed on a banner or
Cried out when one enters the battle is very important.
It represents what the warrior believes to be
The principle of behavior that is most important in life.

In applying this definition to
Spiritual battle, what motto should we use?

We must choose these words in Romans 8:37

"MORE THAN CONQUERORS!"

You are now prepared! Shout the
Christian motto and confront
Your enemy!

Isaiah 42:13
(niv   1984)

The Lord Marches!!

"The Lord will march out like a mighty man,

Like a warrior he will stir up his zeal,

<u>With a shout!!</u>

He will raise the battle cry

And will triumph

Over his enemies"!

Section Two

The Coat of Arms-
Descriptions

(Artistic Creation and Descriptions)

Christian
Coat Of Arms Description
How the Coat of Arms Began

In ancient times, each family developed
Its own unique design of identification.
Symbols were used to depict the family or their
Views and beliefs. Once the design was created,
It was displayed during a battle.
It was usually painted on the shield
Or sewn onto the mantle or flag.
A very prominent place to display it was
On the individual's armor. For this reason
The design was called a Coat Of Arms.

The design created to identify each individual was important.
Because there were so many different ones it became
Necessary for them all to be recorded somewhere. The
Courts gave that job to the heralds. They were to
List each surname and the Coats of Arms that
Went with it. Legally, the King of Arms then
Granted the right for the individual to
Claim that Coat of Arms
As his very own.

Christian
Coat Of Arms Description
Symbols

Jesus, himself, used symbols. There is a rich treasury of symbols
In the Bible that conveys the Christian Message.

Some examples:

(John 15:5) <u>Vine and branches</u>:
"I am the vine, ye are the branches."

(Mark 14:22) <u>The bread</u>:
"Take (the bread), eat; this is my body."

(Mark 14:24) <u>The wine</u>:
"This (Wine) is my blood."

On the following pages, there will be descriptions of each
Symbol used to create the Coat Of Arms,
Along with scriptures that apply.

The Christian Coat of Arms is shown on the back cover of
This book. (If you would like to have a clean colorful
Print of this Coat Of Arms to frame and display,
Identifying yourself as Christian, the order
Information can be found on the
Last page of the book).

Christian
Coat Of Arms Description

Exodus 15:3

"The Lord is

A man of war:

The Lord is

His name."

Christian
Coat Of Arms Description
<u>Crest</u> - Representing Christ

a) *Triumphant Cross = Earth and Cross.*

   (1 John 5:4) "Whatsoever is born of God overcometh the world:
   And this is the victory that overcometh the world, even our faith."

b) *Brass Circles = Eternity.*

   (Romans 6: 23) "...The gift of God is eternal life, through
   Jesus Christ."

c) *The Fish = A Symbol of Christianity.*

   (Matthew 4:19) "...Follow me, and I will make you fishers of men."
   "Ichthus" is the Greek word for fish. The Greek letters for this
   Word - IXOYC- are the first letters from each of the words
   "Jesus Christ, Son of God, Savior."

d) *Resurrection Crosses (2) = Christ is Risen.*

   (Luke 24: 6) "He is not here, but is risen."

e) *Morning Star = A Name Christ Gave to Himself.*

   (Revelation 22:16) "I am...the bright and morning star."

Christian
Coat Of Arms Description
<u>Helmet</u> - Represents Salvation,
(Safety and Soundness)

a) A Brass Helmet= Signifies a Royal Standing.

   (Galatians 4:7) "Wherefore thou art no more a servant, but
   A son; and if a son, then an heir of God through Christ."

b) Brass Visor and Bars = Worn only by Royalty.

   (Luke 2:30) "For mine eyes have seen thy salvation."

c) Facing Straight Forward = Denotes Royal Status.

   (Revelation 22: 4-5) "And they shall see his face...
   And they shall reign for ever and ever."

d) Royal Blue Color = Represents faithfulness.

   (Psalms 31: 23) "For the Lord preserveth the faithful."

e) Safety = "Free from Danger."

   (Luke 21:18) "But there shall not an hair of your head perish."

f) Soundness = "Healthy."

   (II Timothy 1:7) "For God hath not given us the spirit of fear;
   But...a sound mind."

Christian
Coat Of Arms Description
<u>Shield</u> - Represents Our Spiritual Lineage

a) A Brass Shield = Represents Royalty. (Genesis 15:1) "I am thy shield."

b) The Cross = Dividing the four sections, uniting the symbols.
   (John 3:16) "For God so loved the world, that he gave his only
   Begotten Son, that whosoever believeth in him should not
   Perish, but have everlasting life."

c) Alpha/ Omega = Top left quarter, representing God.
   (Revelation 1:8) "I am the Alpha and Omega, the beginning and the
   Ending saith the Lord."

d) Chi Roe = Right quarter, Greek letters representing the title "Christ".
   (I John 4:15) "Whosoever shall confess that Jesus is the Son of God,
   God dwelleth in him, and he in God."

e) Spiritus Sanctus = Bottom left quarter, representing the Holy Spirit.
   (John 14:26) "But the Comforter, which is the Holy Ghost, whom the
   Father will send in my name, he shall teach you all things."

f) Hebrew Marks = Right quarter, representing us;
   We may choose to serve God or to serve his enemy.
           (Genesis 4:1-7) The marks in Hebrew say:
           "Thou shall be it's (sin's) master."

Christian
Coat Of Arms Description
<u>Supporter, Right</u> - Michael –
"Angel of Judgment"

a) He supports and stands with the children of God
    (Daniel 12:1) "And at that time shall Michael stand up,
    The great prince which standeth for the children of thy
    People...and at that time thy people shall be delivered."

b) He fights against Satan and protects God's children.
    (Revelations 12:7) "And there was war in heaven: Michael
    And his angels fought against the dragon (Satan)."

c) Royal Red Color = Symbol for Strength and Might.
    (II Peter 2:11) "Whereas angels, which are greater
    In power and might..."

Christian
Coat Of Arms Description
Supporter, Left - Gabriel –
"The Power of God",
(Herald)

a) *Supporters were used by Royalty = We are Children of God,*
   Thus we are using supporters.
   (Galatians 4:7) "Wherefore thou art no more a servant, but a son;
   And if a son, then an heir of God through Christ."

b) *Supporters = Represent Strength.*
   (Psalms 103:20) "Bless the Lord, ye his angels, that excel in strength."

c) *Supporters Stand in God's Presence = God's Servants.*
   (Luke 1:19) "...I am Gabriel that stands in the presence of God."

Christian
Coat Of Arms Description
Serpent – Represents Satan

I found scriptures about our spiritual enemy in Isaiah, Ezekiel,
And Revelation that will help us to understand him more clearly.

He was an anointed angelic being (Ezekiel 28:14) "Thou are the
Anointed cherub."

He was called: Lucifer, Son of the Morning" (Isaiah 14:12)
"How art thou fallen from heaven, O Lucifer, son of the morning!"

He sinned. (Ezekiel 28:17) "Thou hast corrupted thy wisdom by reason of
Thy brightness. I will cast thee to the ground, I will lay thee before kings,
That they may behold thee."

He was proud. (Ezekiel 28:17a) "Thine heart was lifted up because
Of thy beauty."

He wanted to be greater than God "(Isaiah 14:13 – 14) "For thou hast said
In thine heart, I will ascend into heaven, I will exalt my throne above
The Stars of God: I will sit also upon the mount of the congregation, in
The sides of the north: I will ascend above the heights of the clouds; I will
be Like the Most High."

God cast him out of heaven. (Revelation 12:9) "And the great dragon was
Cast out, that old serpent, called the Devil, and Satan, which deceiveth
The whole world: he was cast out into the earth, and his angels were cast
Out with him." (Note: He is no longer called Lucifer).

He became the Prince of the world (John 14:30) "Hereafter I will
Not talk much with you: for the prince of this world
Cometh, and hath nothing in me."

He seeks to destroy God's people (1 Peter 5:8) "Be sober, be vigilant;

Because your adversary, the devil, as a

Roaring lion, walketh about, seeking

Whom he may devour."

Christian
Coat Of Arms Description

(Serpent Continued)

TAKE HEART, DEAR READER!

The book of Revelation gives three prophecies that tell you that the Time will come when the serpent, that old devil, will be dealt with.

(Revelation 20:1) "And I saw an angel come down from heaven, having The key of the bottomless pit and a great chain in his hand."

(Revelation 20:2) "And he laid hold on the dragon, that old serpent, Which is the Devil, and Satan, and bound him a thousand years."

(Revelation 20:10) "And the devil that deceived them was cast into the Lake of fire and brimstone, where the beast and the false prophet are, And shall be tormented day and night for ever and ever."

And here you find yourself between Lucifer being thrown out of Heaven and the Revelation prophecies being fulfilled.

You have a constant, daily spiritual battle. However, "For though we Walk in the flesh, we do not war after the flesh: For the weapons of Our warfare are not carnal, but mighty through God to The pulling down of strong holds."

(II Corinthians 10:3-4)

Christian
Coat Of Arms Description

(Serpent Continued)

Therefore, Each Day:

1. *Submit yourselves therefore to God. (James 4:7a)*
2. *Resist the devil and he will flee from you."*

(James 4:7b)

"Behold, I give unto you power to tread on serpents
And scorpions, and over all the power of the enemy:
And nothing shall by any means hurt you."

(Luke 10:19)

3. # PUT ON

THE WHOLE

ARMOR OF GOD!

(Ephesians 6:11)

Whole Armor Of God
Bibliography

Chorzempa, Rosemary A. (1987). *Design Your Own Coat of Arms, An Introduction to Heraldry*, 1st ed. Mineola, NY: Dover Publication.

Gouker, Loice. *Dictionary of Church Terms and Symbols, 1st ed.* Norwalk, CT: The C.R. Gibson Company, MCMLXIV.

Hartzell, J. C. (1975). *Your Name, Your Arms, Your Heritage, 1st ed.* Halberts, Inc., Albert E. Deeds Associates, Inc.

Holy Bible, Authorized Version. Philadelphia, PA: The John C. Winston Co.

http://www.wikipedia.org/

KJV Super Giant Print Reference Bible (1996). Nashville, TN: Broadman & Holman Publishers.

THE HOLY BIBLE, New International Version, NIV copyright 1984 by *Biblica, Inc.* TM

Rest, Friedrich (1964). *Our Christian Symbols*, 4th ed. Philadelphia, PA: The Christian Education Press.

Thompson, Frank Charles, D.D., PH.D. (1964). *Chain Reference Bible, King James Version*, 59th ed. Indianapolis, IN: B.B. Kirkbride Bible Co., Inc.

Whole Armor Of God

Bibliography (Continued)

Whittemore, Carroll E. (1984). *Symbols of the Church*, 11th ed. Nashville, TN: Abingdon Press, 1959.

Woodcock, Thomas & Robinson, John Martin 1988). *The Oxford Guide To Heraldry*, 1st ed. Oxford UK: Oxford University Press.

Whole Armor Of God
Biography

Merry was born in Milton, WI in 1940. She is the youngest girl of
Four daughters. She is married to Ron Fitz-Randolph and they reside
In Milton. This is her first book.

Merry loves her God, her Ron, music, nature, art, children, her four sons,
Three daughters, grand-children, great grandchildren, their adopted
Family (the Snyders) and so many other people. She especially enjoys
Helping people when they are hurting or confused.

She uses oils, acrylics and water colors when she paints. She painted
A 3 x 4 foot oil painting and gave it to Mr. and Mrs. Jimmy Carter
Just before they moved into the White House.

She has enjoyed creating greeting cards and restoring photographs on
The computer in days past.

Creating the Universal Coat of Arms for this book has been the greatest
Computer accomplishment, since she created most of it while she was
Going blind. She has macular degeneration.

Whole Armor Of God

Biography (Continued)

This book was many years in the making.

It is Merry's desire that the reader will find knowledge, confidence and stronger faith within the pages of this book.

God is Merry's favorite author and his words will always give us victory. The Bible is his word. Therefore you will find his word throughout this book.

Whole Armor Of God

Prints of the COAT OF ARMS

Can be purchased on line at

<ins>www.mycoatofarms.net</ins>

Eight and a half by eleven

or

Eleven by seventeen

THE WHOLE ARMOR OF GOD!

(Ephesians 6:10 ~ 18)

Author and Illustrator: Merry Sonshine